The FIRST BOOK of
SILVER

First-prize winner of the Sterling Silver Design Competition, these wine cups were designed by Alfred E. Green. The interiors of the cups are washed with gold, and the cast-silver oxidized stems feature raised polished surfaces. (Courtesy Sterling Silversmiths Guild of America)

The FIRST BOOK of
SILVER

by Sara Hannum Chase

Illustrated with photographs

FRANKLIN WATTS, INC.
575 Lexington Avenue
New York, N.Y. 10022

For John Terry

The poetry on page 5 is reprinted with permission of The Macmillan Company, Mr. M. B. Yeats, and the Macmillan Co. of Canada from the poem "The Song of Wandering Aengus," from *Collected Poems* by William Butler Yeats. Copyright 1906 by The Macmillan Company, renewed 1934 by William Butler Yeats.

The author wishes to thank Eastman Kodak Company, Bunker Hill Company, International Silver Company, Sylvania Electrical Products, and Towle Manufacturing Company for their kind co-operation.

Jacket photograph: Ferdinand I (1503–64) silver thaler, courtesy The Metropolitan Museum of Art, gift of George D. Pratt, 1926.

2 3 4 5

CONTENTS

The FIRST BOOK of
SILVER

Reliquary head from the Church of St. Yrieix, France, thirteenth century. (The Metropolitan Museum of Art, Gift of J. Pierpont Morgan, 1917)

INTRODUCTION

Silver has always been a highly prized metal. Silver money has brought men to power, and the lack of silver coins has brought kings to ruin. For thousands of years, craftsmen have made beautiful ornaments of silver. The search for new supplies of silver encouraged men to conquer the New World and later, in the nineteenth century, to brave the dangers of the frontier in the American Far West. In the twentieth century, a rocket could not blast off, a photograph could not be taken, a light could not be switched on without silver.

The Magic Metal

Silver is a very soft metal. It is second only to gold in softness and can be worked into any shape. Silver can be melted down, cooled, and reshaped again. It can be hammered into sheets so thin that it would take 100,000 of them to stack an inch high. Silver can be drawn into a wire finer than a human hair.

Polished silver reflects 95 percent of the light that falls on it. Look at a silver object and watch how it changes in the light. It sparkles in the sunshine; it glows under the soft light of candles.

Silver is the best conductor of electricity and heat. It can withstand high temperatures and does not melt until the temperature has reached almost 961°C. Unlike many metals, silver is unharmed by sudden temperature changes. Also, silver does not *oxidize* easily. That means that the oxygen in the air acts very slowly upon the chemical structure of silver. Iron oxidizes easily and that is why it rusts. But silver does not react with many substances: it is highly resistant to corrosion, and only a few acids can break it down.

1

Silver does react with one substance — sulfur. Silver left in the open will react with the sulfur in the air and turn slightly yellow. This is known as *tarnishing*.

Silver can be alloyed with other metals. An *alloy* is a chemical combination of two or more metals. Silver alloys play an essential part in industry.

Launching of a Saturn spacecraft. (NASA)

Silver is a metal that can be worked easily. The simple style of the porringer, top (made by Peter Van Dyck of New York City about 1704), shows off silver's luster. The silver ship, right (German, about 1744), its rigging, busy crew, and supporting dolphin demonstrate what a multitude of shapes silver can be made into. (The New York Historical Society, New York City [top]; The Metropolitan Museum of Art, Gift of J. Pierpont Morgan, 1917)

Classical Greek silver coins. (The Metropolitan Museum of Art, Gift of J. Pierpont Morgan, 1905)

THE SILVER KINGDOM OF COINS

"The silver apples of the moon, the golden apples of the sun," wrote the Irish poet W. B. Yeats.

Silver is like the pale, shimmering moon, and gold is like the blazing sun. The two metals, like the sun and the moon, have always fascinated man. Silver and gold are found mixed together in the earth, and they have been precious metals ever since their sparkle first caught primitive man's eye thousands of years ago.

From all accounts, silver was first discovered in the land of the Hittites, in the country now known as Turkey. By 3000 B.C., the Hittite silver mines were producing so much silver that the Hittites named their capital city a word that meant "silver."

In that same land, silver was first put to one of its most important uses — it was made into coins. By that time — the seventh century B.C. — the name of the land had been changed to Lydia. In those days there was no money as we know it. People either traded one article for another, or they offered a certain number of cows for what they wanted. Imagine going to market with ten cows to spend! If a person did not spend all his cows, he would have to drive his "change" home, as well as carry the goods he had bought. The Lydians solved this problem by inventing coins and making each coin equal to the value of one cow.

The nearby city-states of Greece saw how practical the Lydians' coins were, and soon the Greeks started making silver coins of their own. The Greeks took their silver from the silver mines in the Laurium Mountains near the city of Athens. The mines were so rich that the Greek playwright Aeschylus called them a "fountain running silver."

Athens' silver coins gave her a leading place among the Greek cities. In 480 B.C., her coins helped to save her from a powerful invader, the Persian king Xerxes.

Xerxes was known as the Great King because his kingdom stretched from India to Egypt. He had a huge army, but more impressive than the soldiers who carried spears and bows and arrows was the Great King's bodyguard. The ancient Greek historian Herodotus wrote that the bodyguard carried magnificent spears tipped with glittering pomegranates of silver and gold.

The people of Athens were frightened when they heard that the Great King was coming. But luck was with them. A new and very rich supply of silver had been found at the Laurium mines. A clever leader named Themistocles had advised the people to spend the silver on building a fleet of warships. Two hundred vessels were now ready to sail against the Persians.

When news came that Xerxes was not far from Athens, all of the Athenians except a small guard fled to safety. Xerxes marched his troops triumphantly into a deserted city. However, things were going very differently at sea. In the famous battle of Salamis, the Greek ships won a victory over Xerxes' navy. Xerxes was defeated, and Athens emerged as a great sea power.

The strength of Athens was partly based on her huge supply of silver coins. In 413 B.C., the slaves at the Laurium mines revolted and joined Sparta, Athens' bitter rival. The supply of silver was

The face of Athena, the goddess of wisdom and the special protector of Athens, was put on many of Athens' silver coins. This coin, a silver tetradrachm from Athens, was made about 429–421 B.C. (The Metropolitan Museum of Art, Gift of Edmund Kerper, 1952)

cut off, and Athens became nearly bankrupt. The proud city was even driven to use copper coins. Not until forty years later did Athens regain possession of the mines. Once again silver coins flowed into Athens. So much silver was minted that the mines were finally exhausted. By 310 B.C., they closed down for good.

When new invaders threatened the Greek cities, the Greeks no longer had the power to fight back. They called on Rome for help. Rome agreed to help, but seized 100,000 silver coins as her price for saving the Greeks. With their treasure chests empty, the Greeks were forced to accept Roman rule.

A Spendthrift Rome Misuses Her Silver Coins

Rome's wealth enabled her citizens to live luxuriously. Wealthy Roman women looked into mirrors made of polished silver. They wore silver earrings and silver necklaces. At fashionable Roman dinners, guests lay on couches made of silver and wood, and toasted each other with wine in silver goblets.

Wealthy Romans looked into mirrors made of polished silver. (The Metropolitan Museum of Art, Rogers Fund, 1907)

There were other luxuries that a man who had enough silver coins in his pocket could buy in Rome's markets. In one stall lions from Africa paced in their cages until they were bought for the arena. Next to their cages a merchant might be offering silk from China or pearls from India. Nearby were piles of grain from England, Spain, and the countries around the Black Sea.

The Romans had thought of every possible luxury, but they had forgotten one very important fact. As they bought all these wonderful goods they spent more and more of their silver. Rome's silver came from the mines of countries she had captured. Most of the silver Rome used came from Spain. But mines do not last forever. Suddenly the Roman government discovered that there was not enough silver left in their mines to pay their bills. The supply of gold was running out, too.

In desperation, the government ordered that all the coins in the country be turned in. The old coins were melted down into new ones. But the new ones did not contain as much gold or silver as the old ones. There was so little real silver in the silver coins that the government demanded that all taxes be paid in gold or goods, even though the people were forced to use the silver coins as money for other purposes.

The inability to handle gold and silver properly was one reason why Rome gradually weakened. Eventually, in A.D. 410, Rome was overrun by barbarian tribes.

Roman coin. (The Metropolitan Museum of Art, Gift of Joseph H. Durkee, 1899)

Too Many Coins Cause Trouble

For a long time after the fall of the Roman Empire, no more silver was mined in Europe. There was a great shortage of silver coins. Instead of looking for new supplies of silver, some rulers pretended they had more silver than they really did. One German king who ruled for thirty-two years called in his silver coins three times a year. Each time he melted down the coins and made cheaper ones that contained less silver. By the end of his rule it was almost a joke to call his coins silver.

To make everything even more confusing, there were hundreds of different kinds of coins in every kingdom in Europe. Nobles, who had the same right as the king to make coins, demanded that their coins be used in the district where they lived. The coins changed every few miles. They were all so worthless that an inn-keeper from one district did not like to be paid in coins from the neighboring district. As for the traveler, he never trusted the coins he was given in change. There was counterfeit money, too. Threats of being boiled alive in oil — the punishment for minting fake coins — did not stop the counterfeiters.

Money became so worthless that trade almost stopped. People grew their own food and made their own clothes. They never left their villages because they had no way to pay for food and lodging and no way to buy and sell goods.

A few kings tried to put an end to this situation. In the ninth century, the emperor Charlemagne gave his people trustworthy silver pennies. After his death, however, all these pennies were melted down and made into cheaper coins.

Finally, two events led to the improvement of silver money in Europe. First, new mines were discovered in Germany. Second, and more important, in 1192 the ruler of Venice, the doge, made

9

Edward I (1272–1307), silver groat.

a new coin. He called it a groat. Every groat contained two grams
of silver. The amount of silver never changed from coin to coin.
The groat was so reliable that it soon became the most popular
coin in Europe. The Venetian craftsmen liked it best of all, because they could sell their wares without being cheated. As long as
they received groats in payment, they knew they had been fairly
paid.

Now that one good coin had been made, the next step was to
find a universal standard for silver. In 1300 the English king,
Edward I, decided to do just that. He called in The Worshipful
Company of Goldsmiths of the City of London. These men were
silver experts. The Worshipful Company of Goldsmiths was so
powerful that it had the right to judge the quality of every silver
article made in England. The king gave the company new and
even more powerful rights — the right to set up a single standard
for English money, and the right to mint this money.

The goldsmiths knew that a pure silver coin would be so soft
that it would soon bend out of shape, so they decided to mix copper with the silver to make the coin stronger. Each of these silver
coins contained 92.5 percent silver. The rest was copper. They
called their coins *sterling,* and from that day to this, all pieces of
silver marked sterling must by law contain 92.5 percent silver.

10

The Search for Silver in the New World

Some of the men who sailed with Columbus returned to Spain and described the riches to be found in the New World. These reports encouraged many Spaniards to seek their fortune in the new lands. In 1517 a Spanish ship sailing in the Caribbean for Cuba was blown off course. When the ship at last found its way to Cuba, the sailors had a strange story to tell. They said they had discovered a new coast and that the natives who lived there believed their ruler was so rich that he had all the silver and gold in the world. Two years later Hernando Cortes set off with a small band to explore the new coast and discover the rich land of its ruler, the Aztec king of Mexico.

The Aztec king, Montezuma, had the Spaniards secretly watched after they landed and began to make their way through his country. Fast runners, acting as scouts for the king, described the Span-

This version of the Spanish conquest of the Aztecs was drawn about 1520-25 by an Aztec Indian. (American Museum of Natural History)

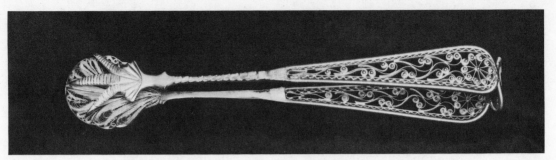

These delicate tongs are an example of the Aztecs' skill in shaping silver. (The New York Historical Society, New York City)

iards and reported their actions. Montezuma was puzzled when he heard what the Spaniards looked like, for the Aztec people believed that one day tall gods with white skin and flowing beards would come to their land. The Spaniards fitted the description exactly.

Montezuma decided there was only one way to find out whether these strangers were gods or men. He planned to send them beautiful presents. If they were gods, they would take his presents as a sign of his respect. If they were men, they would be afraid to attack a ruler who was so rich.

Montezuma sent the Spaniards two huge wheels, one made of silver and the other of gold. One wheel was a picture of the sun and was so large that one man could not carry it. Another present was a bird with gold and silver feathers. But these rich gifts did not have the effect that Montezuma wanted. Instead of being frightened by Montezuma's power, the Spaniards were so excited by the silver and gold that they became greedy. They wanted all of Montezuma's treasure, and they were willing to undergo any danger to get control of his silver and gold mines. It was not long before the Spaniards captured Montezuma and made his people slaves in the mines.

The Incas hid this silver llama with its coat of beaten silver strands from the Spanish. Archaeologists found it hundreds of years later, buried in Inca ruins. (American Museum of Natural History)

Even all the silver and gold of Mexico did not satisfy the Spaniards. From the natives they heard that a land of silver mountains lay to the south. The mountains were the kingdom of the Incas, in what is now Peru. All the silver mined from the mountains belonged to Atahualpa, the king of the Incas. The Incas did not make coins from their gold and silver — they did not use money of any kind. Instead they made beautiful silver and gold ornaments for their king and for their gods.

One Spaniard, Francisco Pizarro, was sure he could discover this fabulous land of the silver mountains. In 1532, he and his party succeeded in finding their way over the steep Andes Mountains into the Inca kingdom.

Atahualpa heard of their arrival and prepared for war. But first he wanted to find out a little more about the men who were clever enough to find his mountain passes, so he invited them into his camp. No harm was done to the Spaniards. The Spaniards then invited Atahualpa to visit them in their camp. Atahualpa trusted them and walked into a trap. Atahualpa was so mighty in the eyes of the people that when the Spaniards captured him, they also captured the fighting spirit of the Incas.

Atahualpa tried to bargain with the Spaniards for his freedom. He promised them that he would fill one room with gold and another twenty times over with silver. He sent messengers throughout his land telling his people to bring to the Spaniards all the treasures from his palace. His people brought gold and silver flowers, and ears of corn with gold kernels and silver tassels, and many other treasures. Although Atahualpa had kept his bargain, the Spaniards sentenced him to death because they suspected him of planning to betray them. After his death, they claimed the Inca kingdom and its silver mines at Potosí as their own.

By 1550, Spain was in complete control of the silver mines of Mexico and Peru. These mines were thousands of miles away from the nearest Spanish ports. After the silver had been mined, it was loaded on llamas in Peru and on mules in Mexico and sent on the treacherous journey to the ports. Spanish ships picked up the loads at the ports and carried the treasure to Cuba. There, twice a year, the huge Spanish galleons came to take the silver and gold back to Spain.

Print showing a wagon loaded with silver, with an armed escort, following the Camino Real, the trail in Mexico that led the Spanish conquistadors from Mexico City to the coast.

Pirate Raids

Although the Spaniards managed to overcome the natives and grow rich on the gold and silver, they were not able to overcome the greatest danger of all — pirates. The first pirate raids in the Caribbean were made by ship captains from England, Holland, and France. These countries were jealous of Spain because she had taken control of the silver and gold in Mexico and Peru. The rulers of these countries gave the ship captains permission to attack the Spanish ships and seize their treasure cargo.

The most daring pirate raid of all took place in September of 1628. The Spanish silver fleet, carrying all the silver from Peru and Mexico, was preparing to sail from Cuba for Spain. Before the Spanish fleet sailed, fast frigates scouted the coastline for pirates. The coast appeared to be quiet, and orders were given for the Spanish silver fleet to leave Cuba. The slow-moving treasure ships were guarded by heavily armed men-of-war. Attack seemed impossible as long as the fleet stayed together.

Suddenly, not one but thirty-one pirate ships came into sight. Piet Heyn, the captain of the pirate fleet, had been given a navy of 700 cannon and 3,000 men by the Dutch government. In addition to this strength, Heyn also had the advantage of surprise.

The Spaniards tried to outsail the pirates and reach the open sea. Heyn's ships were too quick for them, and the Spaniards were driven into a bay, where some of the ships headed up a nearby river for safety. The pirate ships followed, boarded the Spanish ships, and seized the treasure. Not one Spanish ship escaped.

Heyn proudly brought the captured treasure to the Netherlands. He had millions of dollars' worth of silver, most of which he turned over to the Dutch East India Company for use in spreading Dutch colonization in the Far East.

16

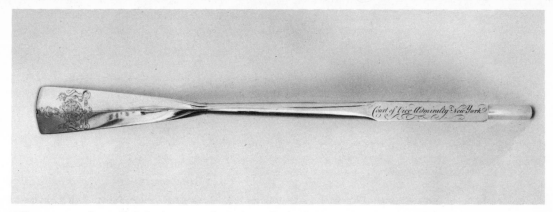

Silver oar, the official sign of the vice-admiralty court. (Lent to the Museum of the City of New York by the United States District Court for the Southern District of New York)

By 1698, pirates were no longer heroes to the English, the French, and the Dutch. These countries had made peace with Spain, and they wanted the pirates to stop their raids. William III, the king of England, was so eager to put an end to pirates that he had a new piece of silver made just for them. The silver was shaped like an oar and measured 28 inches long. The oar was the official sign of the vice-admiralty court. Any colonial officer who had the oar had the right to try pirates wherever he found them and to hang them if they were found guilty. The oar was carried before the judge who came to try the pirates and was placed in front of him as the trial began. The silver oar was often the last piece of silver a pirate saw.

The First American Coins

When the colonists came to settle in the New World, they brought with them as much silver as they could. They had English coins, Dutch coins, French coins, and Spanish coins. These coins made up their fortunes, and they worried about being robbed.

17

The colonial silversmith Samuel Tingley made this tankard for Philip S. Van Rensselaer. A thief would have thought twice before stealing a tankard with such an easily recognizable design. (The New York Historical Society, New York City)

To protect themselves, the colonists asked the silversmiths to melt their coins down and fashion household objects from them. Often, they had the silversmith put an unusual decoration or a long inscription on the silver. If the object was stolen, the owner placed its description in the newspaper. When the thief tried to sell the stolen goods, the inscription on the silver gave him away. He was caught, and the silver was returned to the owner. People were so convinced that it was safer to have their silver made into objects that debts were often paid with a silver candlestick or a cup.

The silversmiths were very important people because they were trusted with people's silver. Everyone thought of them as bankers. When the time came for the colonies to mint their own money, the governor of Massachusetts turned to two of the most respected silversmiths in Boston, John Hull and Robert Sanderson, and asked them to mint the colony's money. To show their love of their new land, they chose the native pine trees as the decoration for the money. These coins, first made in 1652, came to be called the pine tree shillings.

Right: *Instead of melting down the silver, some coins were fitted into spoons. This spoon, a silver military Communion spoon, was made from two coins from the reign of George II (1727–60.)* (The New York Historical Society, New York City)

Below: *Pine tree shillings.* (The Metropolitan Museum of Art, Bequest of A. T. Clearwater, 1933)

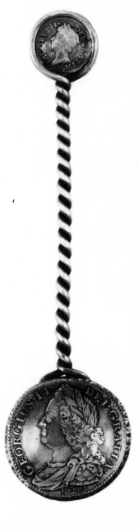

The Story of the Silver Dollar

In 1792, Alexander Hamilton, Secretary of the Treasury for the new United States government, issued both a gold and a silver dollar. Although silver dollars stayed in circulation, the gold dollar was always more popular.

In 1873, Congress passed a new coinage law that stated the exact amount of gold that must be in a gold dollar but said nothing about the amount of silver needed for a silver dollar. No more silver dollars were going to be coined.

This new law passed unnoticed at first because the miners were busy selling their silver to the highest bidder. Then a depression hit the country. The price of silver dropped. Now the miners wanted to sell their silver to the government, but they discovered that the government did not want it. The miners began to call the new coinage act the "crime of '73." People who were out of work joined with the miners. They wanted silver dollars. The country was divided into "goldbugs," who believed that there should only be gold dollars, and "silverites," who were fighting to bring back silver dollars.

The Presidential campaign of 1896 was a bitter fight between the goldbugs and the silverites. William Jennings Bryan took the side of silver and waged a very dramatic and forceful campaign against the goldbug candidate, William McKinley. But Bryan could not carry the country — McKinley and the goldbugs won. It looked like the end of the silver dollar, but the silverites did not give up and, finally, the Silver Purchase Act of 1934 authorized the government to buy a certain amount of silver every year for silver dollars.

In 1946, the United States treasury had more silver in its stockpile than it needed for silver dollars. Although the government did not need the silver, industry did, for silver had become a vital industrial material. The government offered silver to industry for $1.29 an ounce, and for several years all seemed well. Suddenly, the government was facing a severe shortage of silver coins. It investigated the disappearance of the coins but could find no satisfactory answer. One belief was that coins were taken out of circulation by vending machines. However, it was pointed out that vending machines were regularly emptied and the coins put back in circulation. Another explanation was that people were hoarding coins. Some were coin collectors. Others were holding the coins in expectation of a rise in the price of silver. They planned to sell their hidden stock of coins when the price went up. Whatever the cause, the government tried to correct the shortage by asking the public not to hoard coins and to give exact change. The campaign helped, but not enough coins came back in circulation.

The government had to dip into its stockpile of silver, and mint more coins. From 1953 to 1963, the United States was coining 60 percent of the free world's coinage. It soon became clear that the supply of silver would not hold out if the mint continued to make so many new coins. In 1965, the government passed a coinage act that drastically lowered the amount of silver in coins. All dimes and quarters coined in the future would contain no silver. The silver in fifty-cent pieces dropped from 90 percent to 40 percent.

Still, the government continued to hold the price of silver for industry at $1.29 an ounce. However, in 1967, the government dropped its curb and left the price of silver to be decided on the open market. The price soared from $1.29 to $1.81. Today the price changes daily depending on the demand for silver. This means more expenses for those industries that need silver, and it also threatens the life of the old silver coins. As soon as the silver in a coin becomes more valuable than the coin itself, people may melt the coins and sell the silver at the current market price. This is a very dangerous thing. Silver in coins can be used again and again. No matter how often the coin changes hands, the silver is still there. When coins are melted and the silver is sold, the silver is gone and the known supply of silver in the world is that much lower. The government has tried to protect coins by setting up a penalty for anyone caught melting coins. A person who melts coins can be fined $10,000 and receive a jail sentence of five years. But even with such protection, silver coins may become a thing of the past.

Bidding on silver. (The New York Times)

These three silver canisters belonged to the Egyptian pharaoh, Thutmose III (1501–1447 B.C.*). The names of his wives, Merty, Menwy, and Menhet, are cut into the silver in hieroglyphics.* (The Metropolitan Museum of Art, Rogers Fund, 1917)

THE CRAFT OF SILVER

Man began to work with silver as soon as it was discovered. Little by little, he learned how to hammer the metal into the shape he wanted. Examples of the art of early silversmiths have been found in the tombs of the pharaohs. This was because the Egyptian people believed that the dead would need clothing, furniture, and food in the afterlife. When someone died, his favorite possessions were buried with him. Archaeologists have discovered delicate silver jewelry and other silver objects in the tombs of the pharaohs.

Perhaps the best silver craftsmen in the ancient world were the Romans. No design was too difficult for the expert hand of a Roman silversmith. He worked silver into every imaginable shape. Not long ago a silver head depicting a Roman emperor was found in northern Italy. Every detail of the emperor's face had been captured in the silver. Although the craftsman hammered the head out of silver almost two thousand years ago, and even though the silver head had been buried for many years, it is as perfect today as when it was first made.

The figures of this hunting scene, hammered out of silver by a Roman craftsman of the second century A.D., *actually seem to be moving.* (The Metropolitan Museum of Art, Rogers Fund, 1906)

There have been master craftsmen in all periods of history, and each of these men has a story. But it is impossible to study all of the gifted silversmiths here. We can, however, look at three periods of history and see what the silversmiths did to earn their fame.

Benvenuto Cellini Makes a Silver Jupiter

Benvenuto Cellini was born in Florence, Italy, in 1500. By the time he was nineteen, he had gone to Rome to prove that he was the greatest craftsman of his time. Within a few years, he had made his vow come true. Cellini became the best sculptor, goldsmith, and silversmith in all of Rome, and of Italy, too.

Francis I, the king of France, heard about Cellini's amazing skill and asked him to come to France. When Cellini arrived, the first task the king set for him was to make twelve silver candlesticks. He asked Cellini to make each candlestick in the shape of a different god or goddess and asked that each candlestick be as tall as the king.

Many craftsmen would have thought the king's idea of gigantic candlesticks an impossible one. But Cellini thought nothing was

Engraving showing Benvenuto Cellini in his studio. (The Bettmann Archive)

impossible for him. He chose the god Jupiter for the first candlestick. Jupiter was the god of thunder and the king of the gods, so Cellini planned to have the silver Jupiter hold a thunderbolt in his raised right hand and a globe of the world in his left.

When Cellini finished the candlestick, it was so large and shaped so much like a man that it looked almost like a statue. Cellini decided to make the silver Jupiter even more unusual. He put four wooden balls under the statue so that the Jupiter rolled when it was pushed. The Jupiter was now ready to be shown at court.

Cellini had worked so hard to make his Jupiter beautiful for the king that he did not notice he was making enemies at court. One woman in particular, Madame d'Étampes, was furious because Cellini had paid no attention to her. She set out to ruin him.

Madame d'Étampes had a plan. As soon as Cellini arrived with the Jupiter, she sent word for him to take it to a certain room and wait there for the king. When Cellini walked into the room, he discovered that it was full of beautiful bronze statues. They were all new and the king had not yet seen them. Madame d'Étampes thought that when the king saw all the bronze statues, he would not notice one silver candlestick. The hours went by, and soon it was dark. The room was not well lighted — another part of Madame d'Étampes's plan, for she was sure the silver would not show up well in the dim light.

At last the king and his courtiers arrived. They could not believe their eyes as they walked into the room. All they could see was light flashing over the silver Jupiter. The god was holding a burning torch that Cellini had cleverly set in the middle of the silver rays of the thunderbolt. And more than that, the Jupiter was slowly moving toward the king. As the silver Jupiter rolled back and forth on the wooden balls, it almost seemed alive. Madame d'Étampes's trick had failed. The king thought that the Jupiter was the finest thing in the room, and Cellini became the king's favorite craftsman.

The Huguenots

The great French king Louis XIV lived about one hundred and fifty years after Francis I. Louis XIV loved beautiful things, too, and he wanted to build a palace at Versailles, near Paris, that would outshine every palace in Europe. He planned to decorate the palace with the best art of every kind. He ordered one set of furniture that was to be made out of nothing but silver. His table was to be set with silver, and candles in silver candlesticks were to light his rooms.

In order to carry out the king's dream, Jean Baptiste Colbert, the king's minister, organized an arts center. Colbert asked craftsmen from every part of Europe to come and work for Louis XIV. At the arts center, hundreds of silversmiths used their skill to make silver furniture, boxes, and table settings for the king. Soon all of the best silversmiths in Europe were gathered at Versailles.

Many of the craftsmen were Huguenots, the name given to the

The delicate designs on this tea caddy are the work of one of the most famous French Huguenots, Paul Lamerie. He fled to England where his skill as a silversmith helped to make London the center of fine silver craft. (The Metropolitan Museum of Art, Rogers Fund, 1913)

Protestants in France. Some people at court thought the king should force the Huguenots to become Catholics. In 1685, the king gave in to the demands of his courtiers, and told the Huguenots that it now was against the law to be Protestant. But even though they were surrounded by enemies, the Huguenots would not give up their beliefs. The king's soldiers took away their homes and tortured the Huguenots. Many of the Huguenots managed to escape to Holland and England, where they received a welcome and refuge.

It was a mistake to force the Huguenot craftsmen to leave France. After they left, their workshops were empty, and they paid no more taxes to the king. Louis XIV needed money desperately and did not know where to find any now that the workshops had closed down. He looked sadly at the silver furniture and gave a new order. He told his men to load the furniture onto carts and drive to the

Silver coffeepot made in England in 1769–70 combines French and English styles. (The Metropolitan Museum of Art, Gift of Harriett Hunter Sedgwick and Rachel Sedgwick, 1922)

royal mint. There the furniture was melted down and made into coins to pay his majesty's debts.

As for the Huguenots, they used their skills to enrich their new homes. England's greatest period of silver craft began with the arrival of the Huguenots. English silver from that period is highly prized for its delicate design and perfect workmanship.

Many Huguenots found their way to America. One of these men was the father of Paul Revere.

The Liberty Bowl

Paul Revere's ride to warn the people at Lexington that the British were coming made him very famous. But he deserves fame for more than this ride. He was an excellent silversmith.

Paul's father taught him how to be a silversmith. As father and son worked together, the boy heard many stories about what happened to the Huguenots when the king made their religion unlawful. When Paul became a man, he feared that the English king might take away his rights just as the French king had taken away the rights of the Huguenots. The British kept a watchful eye on any man who spoke too freely. They forced the colonists to pay high taxes. In 1763, a man in England named John Wilkes wrote a strong article against these acts of the British in the forty-fifth issue of his newspaper, *The North Briton*. The British answered by putting Wilkes in jail. The colonists were shocked and furious, and "Number Forty-five" became a patriotic cry in Boston.

In 1768, the Massachusetts House of Representatives sent out a letter to all the colonies asking them to protest against the king's unfair laws. The king demanded that the Massachusetts representatives rescind their letter. By a vote of 92 to 17 the representatives refused. Like Wilkes, they were in danger of being put in prison.

Paul Revere's Liberty Bowl. (Museum of Fine Arts, Boston)

The people of Boston admired the courage of the representatives and talked of "The Ninety-two" as well as "Number Forty-five." Paul Revere made a beautiful silver bowl to commemorate these actions. The bowl became known as the Sons of Liberty bowl. One side of the bowl was dedicated to the "Glorious Ninety-two," and "Wilkes and Liberty" was cut into the silver on the other side. The bowl was kept in the Massachusetts House of Representatives as a reminder of the struggle against the British.

Training a Silversmith

From the twelfth century almost to the present day, a man who wanted to be a silversmith had to go through an elaborate system of training. He could not just put a sign over his door and set up shop as a silversmith. All the silversmiths belonged to a group called a guild, and the guild had a strict set of rules for membership.

This engraving is part of the frontispiece from the book called The Touchstone *and shows the silversmiths at work. In one corner, the silver goes into the melting pot. At the back of the shop, silversmiths hammer silver.*

Graceful silver water-pitcher made for President James Madison (1751–1836). (The New York Historical Society, New York City)

A person who wanted to be a silversmith had to begin his training while he was a boy. First, he was *bound* to a master silversmith for seven years. That meant that the boy promised to serve the master faithfully, to do any work that was asked of him, and not to tell anyone the secrets of his master's skill. The master, in turn, promised to give the boy food and a place to sleep, to send him to school at night, and most important of all, to teach him how to become a master craftsman.

The boy had a severe test to pass after he had learned the trade. He was put in a separate room in the hall where the silver guild met, given tools and a piece of silver, and told to produce a masterpiece — a silver object that he made all by himself. If the finished piece was well designed and well made, the boy could call himself a master and take up the silversmith's trade. If it was not, he had to return to his training or try another profession.

There was much for a boy to learn during the seven years of training. Instead of going to a store to choose a silver pattern, a customer went to a silversmith and explained to him what he wanted. The silversmith listened to the customer's ideas, and then he designed a model in clay. If the customer liked the design, he brought his coins or old silver to be melted down.

After the silver was melted into a flat piece, it was heated, or *forged*, and pounded with a hammer until it was the right thickness and strength. Then the silversmith cut out a circular piece from the silver and began to shape it by delicately hammering it into the desired form. This was called *raising*. Sometimes, the silversmith held the silver over a hollow wooden block and pounded the silver sheet, or *plate*, into the hollow. This is how pitchers, coffeepots, and basins were made. Because they were hollow inside, they were and still are called *hollow ware*. Other pieces were called *flatware*.

Elm stump used by two colonial silversmiths, the Moulton brothers, for raising silver. The silversmiths' hammers lie beside the stump. (Towle Manufacturing Company)

The silversmith had to pound every inch of the silver six or eight times to force it into the right shape. Each stroke of the hammer made the silver more brittle and more likely to snap. To keep the silver soft, the silversmith heated it from time to time. This was called *annealing.*

When the piece was shaped, the silversmith put on small parts such as handles, feet, and spouts. These parts were usually cast in molds. Melted silver was poured in the mold where it hardened, and was then fused or soldered onto the main form.

The greatest part of the silversmith's art was in decorating the finished pieces. There were three main kinds of silver decorating — *chasing, engraving,* and *piercing.* Each style called for a special set of tools and a master's touch.

This goblet, made in China and presented to William Wetmore Cryder in 1856, is a fine example of the art of chasing. (The New York Historical Society, New York City)

Chasing was done by pushing the silver into shape without cutting away any of the silver. If a chaser was working on a hollow piece, he first used a *snarling iron*. The snarling iron was a long bar with a tiny hammer on one end. The silversmith put the snarling iron inside the hollow silver piece and gently tapped the iron. Each tap made the hammer vibrate against the silver and pushed it out into a bulge. Before the silversmith pounded the details into the bulges, he filled the silver piece with pitch so that the silver would not lose its shape as it was being worked. Then, using a hammer and a pointed tool called a punch, he slowly forced the bulge into whatever design he wanted. Under the patient hand of a chaser, dancing couples appeared on a bowl or a garland of ribbons circled the edge of a tray.

Engraving was just as beautiful and took just as much skill. An engraver cut his design into the silver. One slip of his sharp-edged tool and the piece was ruined, because there is no way to put back silver that has been cut away. The engraver had hundreds of

The methods of piercing and engraving were used to decorate this early-nineteenth-century fish knife. Two different types of piercing were used to make the double border; the fish is engraved. (The New York Historical Society, New York City)

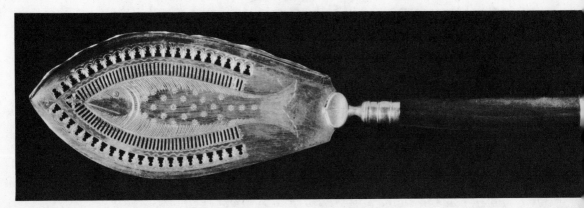

tools from which to choose. With the double edge of a tool called a *bright-cut,* he cut a letter and polished it at the same time. He had to know just what tool to choose to make a fancy twisted initial, to dot an *i,* or to create a rose.

Piercing was another way that silver was cut out. The piercer used a series of punches to make holes in the silver. Often so much of the silver was cut away that the pattern had a lacelike look.

No wonder a boy had to be an apprentice for seven years. Some silver pieces were very simple, but others called for engraving, chasing, and piercing. An early silversmith's book called *The Touchstone,* published in 1677, listed fifty-four tools a silversmith should own, and the list did not include all the tools a chaser or an engraver might have needed.

The Meaning of Hallmarks

Hallmarks are official identification marks that tell a buyer three things about silver — that the silver is sterling, who made the silver, and when it was made. Once hallmarks were used by silversmiths in all countries, but today hallmarks are put on only English silver. In the United States, the sterling stamp and the company name are very much like hallmarks.

The first hallmark was used at the time when The Worshipful Company of Goldsmiths made sterling the official standard for silver. To make sure that all silver pieces were sterling as the law ordered, silversmiths had to have their finished silver stamped with a seal shaped like a leopard's head. The mark of the leopard's head was a safeguard for the buyer. Some thieves treated copper, brass, and lead with arsenic and then tried to peddle the bleached metal as silver. This false silver could not stand the test of the leopard's-head mark, and usually the thieves were caught.

In 1363, a law was passed that required that another mark be added. The silversmiths had to find a mark of their own to identify their work. Some silversmiths took their mark from the shop signs over their doors. They cut a grasshopper or rose or whatever design was on their shop signs into their finished silver. From 1739 on, silversmiths have been required to use the initials of their first and last names as their mark. This so-called *maker's mark* is the personal sign of a silversmith and is like an artist's signature on his painting.

Hallmarks tell a story. Set of initials (right) show that John Wakelin and William Taylor made the piece of silver. Letter k indicates that it was finished between 1785-86. Style of the lion passant *next to the k also helps identify the period. Crowned leopard's head means the silver is sterling. Head of the king, George III, is stamped at far left to prove that the silversmiths paid the silver tax. Figures above the hallmarks show weight of the silver.* (The Metropolitan Museum of Art, Gift of William Rhinelander Stewart, 1926)

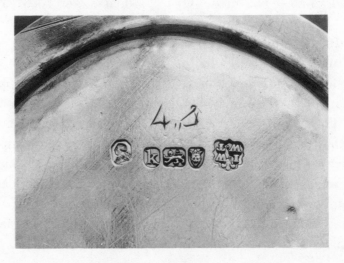

The third mark is a *datemark*. Silver pieces began to be dated in 1478 with an unusual alphabet system beginning with *A*, skipping *J*, and ending with *U*. Each letter stood for a year. After twenty years, the silversmiths started with *A* again. To show the difference between the twenty-year cycles, each set of letters was shaped differently. Imagine all the many kinds of *A*'s there have been since 1478.

Another mark, a *lion passant*, or a lion standing on two feet with his head turned, was first put on silver in 1544. Authorities believe that the silversmiths used this mark to distinguish their true silver from the falsely marked coins of the day.

THE MANUFACTURE OF FINE SILVER TODAY

The craft of making hollow and flat silverware is a great industry today. Many of the steps that were once done by hand are now done by machine, but the craftsman is still very important.

Creating a Pattern

The story of the manufacture of silver objects begins in the design room, where trained artists use their imagination and their talent to create new designs. They may try out a dozen ideas before they find a pattern that pleases them. Many patterns that look exciting on the drawing board are not right for silver. For instance, an artist who wants to create a flower pattern must imagine how the flowers will look when they are shaped out of silver. The flowers may look too crowded. They may not be delicate and graceful enough to fit on the slim handle of a spoon.

When the designer has finished a pattern, he turns it over to a

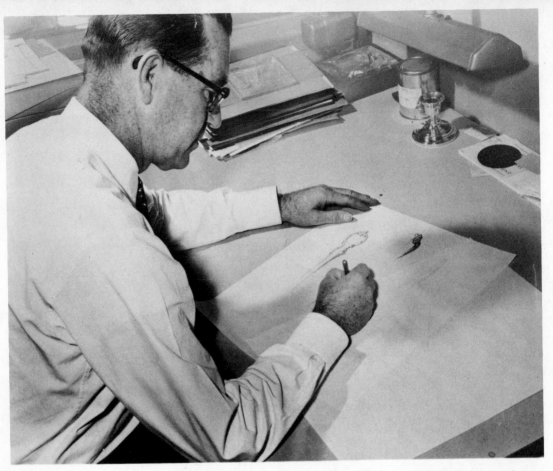

Trained artists create silver designs. (International Silver Company)

master craftsman. The craftsman is the first to put the design on silver. Using the many tools of his trade, he shapes the silver just as the early silversmiths did. Each blow of the hammer on the punch brings the design to life. It may take a craftsman three weeks to put all the details of a drawing onto the trial piece of silver. If the design is a success, the craftsman has made the master copy.

The next step is to make an oversize bronze copy of the pattern and send it to the mold shop. In the mold shop, the long metal finger of the mold-making machine runs carefully over every part of the design in the bronze mold. As the metal finger moves, it forces another metal finger with a sharp edge to cut the pattern into a steel mold. The details of the pattern are put into the steel mold by hand. Trained chasers and engravers add the highlights to the pattern and perfect the mold.

A master chaser uses a hammer and punch to push the silver into the shape of the design. The soft pitch on which the fork is resting keeps the silver from bending out of shape. (International Silver Company)

Machines punch the blanks into shape. (International Silver Company)

Manufacturing the Silver

To make flatware, strips of sterling silver are fed into a machine that cuts them into *blanks*. Blanks have the rough shape of the finished piece of silver. Heavy rollers press the silver blanks into the right length, width, and thickness. Next a stamping machine punches the shape into the blanks. Other machines cut prongs in forks and push out the bowls of spoons.

The blanks are now ready for the steel pattern molds. The molds are fastened to a machine called a drop, or punch, press. The drop press falls with the heavy force of 1,000 pounds and presses the pattern into the silverware. The blanks are fed to the drop press by a worker who must time his movements to the rhythm of the press.

A drop press strikes the design onto the front and back of the handle. (International Silver Company)

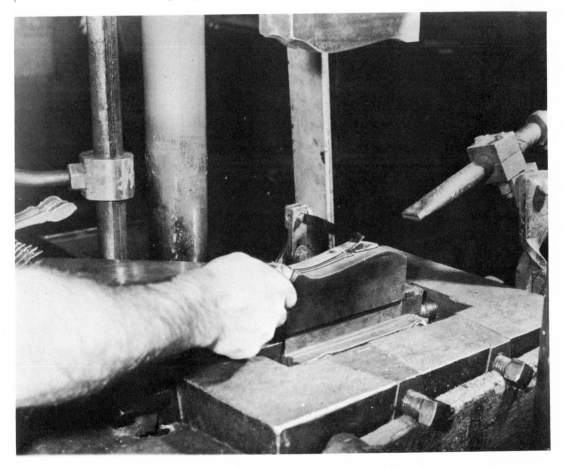

Some patterns are finished by hand. The frosted look of one modern design is made by hundreds of tiny lines cut into the silver. A craftsman runs the silver under a cutting wheel. He must let the silver just barely touch the wheel or the cuts will be too deep. It takes an artist's eye and a steady hand to create this pattern.

Hollow ware is made in several different ways. Sometimes the melted silver is poured into molds where the drop press forces the silver into the mold's shape. Another way to make hollow ware is to stamp out two separate pieces of silver and then solder them together. Knife handles are made in this way.

Generally, different parts of hollow-ware pieces are made separately. Each part is stamped with a pattern, then all the parts are soldered together. For instance, the body, handle, spout, feet, and lid of a coffeepot are all made separately.

Silver cannot be quickly moved from manufacturing step to manufacturing step. Each time the silver is worked on, it must be carefully cleaned and annealed. If the silver were not softened by heating, it would snap under the pressure of the tools.

Finishing the Silver

The silver is then polished and the rough edges are smoothed by a buffing wheel. Some polishing processes used today give the silver a special finish that keeps it from tarnishing quickly. If the pattern has a raised design, it is dipped in an acid bath that darkens the silver. When the silver is polished, the raised parts become very lustrous while the cutout parts remain dark. This contrast of light and dark makes the pattern stand out.

Each piece of silver is checked to see that the pattern is exact and that there are no flaws. One method of inspecting hollow ware is to hold it up against white gauze, where even tiny imperfections

Top: *A high-speed revolving belt rubs the surface of the silver until it is very smooth.* (International Silver Company)

Bottom: *Every piece of silver is carefully inspected for flaws.* (International Silver Company)

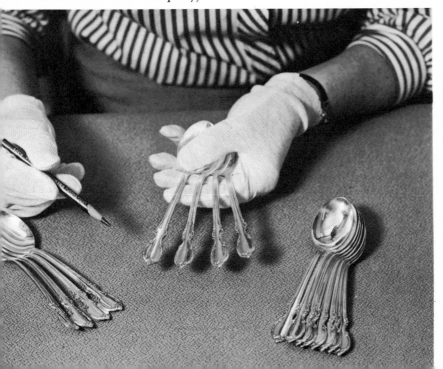

show up clearly. Silver that is not perfect is sent back to a special department. There bumps are pounded out, and parts are resoldered. If the silver cannot be repaired, it is melted down so that it can be used again.

Not a scrap of silver is wasted. The metal is so precious that bits and pieces left by the pattern-stamping machines are gathered up. Even more surprising, silver is salvaged from the factory floor itself. If a room in a silver plant needs a new floor, the old floor is burned and the scraps of silver that may have fallen to the floor are recovered from the ashes.

Silver that has passed inspection is wrapped and sealed in special bags. The bags keep the silver from tarnishing and it comes to the buyer's hands as sparkling as it was when it left the factory.

Napkin holders of the most amazing shapes and styles became popular with the invention of silver plate. (International Silver Company)

THE STORY OF SILVER PLATE

Silver plate is not made of sterling silver. Instead, nickel silver, a metal made up of 65 percent copper, 17 percent zinc, and 18 percent nickel, is covered by a layer of pure silver. Silver plate is as beautiful as sterling, but because it is not all silver, it does not last as long. It is much cheaper, however.

The story of silver plate began with an accident that happened in 1742 to an English knife maker named Thomas Bolsover. One day, while Bolsover was working on a copper knife, drops of melted silver fell on the knife and united with the copper. To Bolsover's surprise, the silver stuck firmly to the knife and he could not get it off. Bolsover soon turned from knife making to selling his gleaming silver-covered copper. People were delighted with his invention, and they came to call it *Sheffield plate* because Bolsover came from Sheffield.

Almost a hundred years later, another Englishman, George Richards Elkington, succeeded in using electricity to plate copper with silver. His method was called *electroplating*. Because silver could be electroplated so quickly and cheaply, electroplating soon replaced Sheffield plate.

Electroplating was first tried in the United States by the Rogers brothers. Their shop was a very simple one. In it was a tub that they filled with a solution of cyanide. A bar of silver was hung in one end and a cup made of nickel silver in the other end. The brothers connected a wire to the bar of silver and another wire to the cup and started an electric current that passed cyanide from the bar to the cup. As the cyanide in the tank dissolved the silver, the electric current forced the silver onto the cup. At the end of this process the silver bar completely disappeared while the cup became coated with a solid layer of silver.

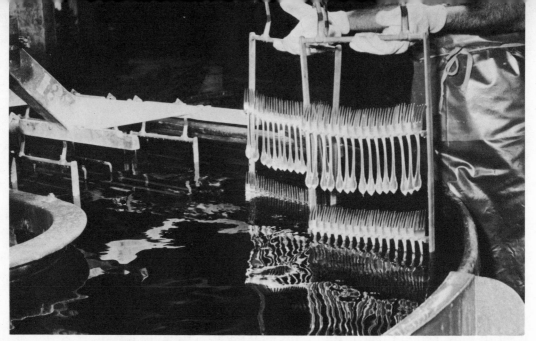

Rack of forks being lowered into an electroplating tank. The stronger the current and the longer the forks stay in the tank, the heavier the coating of silver. (International Silver Company)

A Yankee peddler named Horace Wilcox heard rumors of the Rogers brothers' new silver plate. He investigated the rumor and was amazed to see the silver move mysteriously from the bar to the cup. He loaded his peddler's cart with the silver plate and set out to try his luck in the Connecticut countryside. Along with pots and pans, buttons and scissors, and a host of other household goods, Wilcox offered his shiny silver plate. The silver plate was such a success that he and the Rogers brothers formed a partnership. Silver-plating had begun as a business.

Today, silver plate is very popular. It is treated just like sterling silver and goes through the same manufacturing steps. After the design has been pressed into the nickel silver and the parts have been put together, the nickel silver goes to the electroplating tanks which are filled with cyanide and a silver solution.

The nickel silver is first placed on racks and then immersed in the cleaning tanks. If the nickel silver is not completely clean, the silver solution will not stick to it properly. Then the racks move onto the first of the plating tanks. Each time the racks come out of a plating tank, the layer of silver on the base is thicker.

Because the silver used is pure, it is very soft and will slowly wear away. In fine silver plate, an extra layer of silver is put on the spots that will get the most wear. For instance, the backs of forks and the bowls of spoons are given a thicker coating to make them last longer.

Caring for Silver and Silver Plate

Each time silver is used it takes on a richer glow. Even the tiny network of scratches that comes from use adds to silver's luster because the scratches create more surface for the light to play on.

These spoons, made in 1765, grow more beautiful with every year. Careful handling and attention have given the silver a rich patina. (The New York Historical Society, New York City)

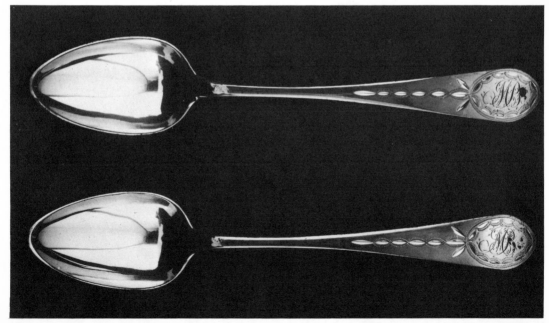

This mellow, shimmering look of old silver is called a *patina*. People have only recently come to understand the value and beauty of silver that is hundreds of years old. It used to be the fashion to melt down old silver and have it shaped to the latest style. Many fine old pieces were lost this way. Even if a family did not melt down the silver, they often sold it during hard times or they were forced to hand their silver over to the government to be melted down for coins. This is why there are very few silver pieces dating before 1700.

The best way to care for silver is to use it often and carefully wash and dry it after each use. Tarnish can be removed by polishing silver with a good silver polish. Polishing takes off a tiny layer of silver as well as the tarnish, so a polish that is not too strong must be used so that as little silver as possible is removed. Silver will not tarnish as quickly if it is kept in felt bags or protective plastic coverings when it is not in use.

Silver religious objects that were kept safely protected in monasteries are almost the only silver that have survived from before 1700. This cross was made by Carolingian silversmiths in France between 700 and 800. (The Metropolitan Museum of Art, Gift of J. Pierpont Morgan, 1917)

THE IMPORTANCE OF SILVER IN INDUSTRY

The greatest use of silver is in photography. When you look at a photograph, you are actually seeing millions of tiny silver specks. Silver salts, a chemical compound of silver with fluorine, chlorine, bromine, or iodine, are sensitive to light. When light strikes paper coated with silver salts, the light rays dissolve the compound and leave tiny bits of metallic silver. Since light rays bounce from one object to another, the bits of metallic silver mirror whatever the light rays first struck. The word "photography" itself means "light writing," and the key to photography is a light-sensitive substance — silver salts; a base — film; and a method to stop the action of the light rays on the silver salts — a developer.

The first person to show that sunlight acts on silver salts was a German professor, Johann Heinrich Schulze. In 1725, he used sunlight to write letters on a solution of silver salts. Schulze knew that silver salts sometimes darken, and he suspected that sunlight was the cause. To prove his theory, he cut out letters from a piece of paper and wrapped the paper around a bottle containing silver salts. Sure enough, the sunlight darkened all the exposed parts and dark letters were clearly printed on the liquid.

Schulze's experiment pointed the way toward photography. In 1802, an Englishman named Thomas Wedgwood succeeded in using the sun's effect on silver salts to form a picture. He made prints of leaves and insects by placing them on paper coated with silver salts and exposing the paper to sunlight. Wedgwood's prints were indeed exact copies of the leaves and insects, but he had one serious problem. He had to look at his prints in candlelight. The instant the prints were put in strong light, the light began to act on the

original negative

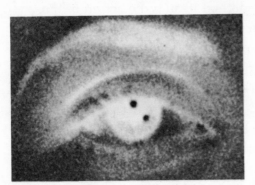

enlarged 25 times

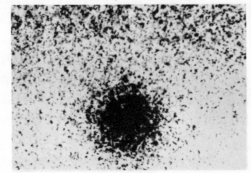

enlarged 250 times

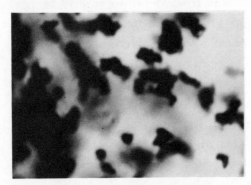

enlarged 2,500 times

enlarged 25,000 times

A negative is made up of tiny grains of black metallic silver. The series of enlargements above show what the grains of silver look like when they are magnified many times.

undissolved silver salts and to turn the entire picture dark.

Joseph Niépce, a Frenchman, solved this difficulty by washing his exposed prints in a nitric acid bath until all the undissolved silver salts were washed away. Niépce deserves the credit for taking the first photograph (in 1826) and for being the first to "fix" his picture so that it would not blacken. Niépce's picture of his courtyard can still be seen today.

How Film Is Made Today

Film is made up of two parts — the silver-salt coating, called an *emulsion*, and the film base. The two parts are prepared separately by a team of technicians who must take special care to keep themselves, their tools, and their ingredients spotlessly clean. Not only must everything around the silver salts be clean, but the technician must work with the salts in the dark. One bright ray of light would start a chemical action in the salts that would spoil them for photography.

First, silver bars are dissolved in nitric acid. Then, the liquid silver is pumped into 1,000-gallon tanks where it is cooled and stirred until it forms crystals.

The emulsion is made up of silver salts and gelatin. The silver salts are mixed in silver-lined tanks, and only the dimmest light helps the technician see what he is doing. The gelatin and the silver nitrate are dissolved in warm water. Potassium bromide and potassium iodine are mixed with the silver nitrate until a chemical reaction takes place and silver salts are formed. Because other chemicals as well as silver salts form in the solution, the emulsion is chilled to a jelly, shredded into long threads, and washed until the unwanted chemicals are gone.

Specially prepared chemicals are now added to the film. These chemicals control the length of time the film must be exposed be-

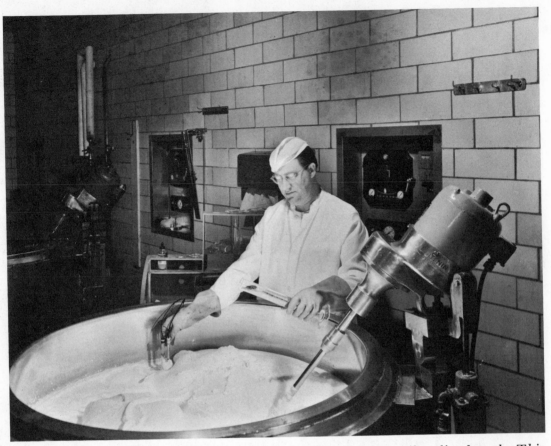

A technician mixes the coating for film in a silver-lined tank. This coating, called an emulsion, is made up of silver salts and gelatin.

fore a picture is recorded. They keep the picture from becoming fuzzy and they make sure that different colors have the same effect on the silver salts. How many and what kind of chemicals are added to the emulsion depends upon the use the film is designed for. There are at least 265 different kinds of emulsions.

As the roll of film unwinds, liquid emulsion of just the right thickness is spread on the film.

The emulsion is ready at last to be coated on the film. The coating is done by machines that spread exactly the right amount of emulsion on the film. Some emulsion coatings are so thin that they are one-tenth the size of a strand of hair. Besides making sure that the machine is coating the film accurately, the technician must take care that no dust falls on the film. The room where he works is vacuumed every day and the air is filtered. The technician himself wears special clothing that cannot pick up specks of dirt.

Color film must be made even more carefully. Many color films are made up of different layers, and each layer is coated with emulsion. One widely used film is made up of the three primary colors, yellow, red, and blue. By the time light has passed through each layer, all the different colors are recorded on the emulsion.

When the film has been coated, it is chilled until the emulsion hardens. Then it is dried and wound into rolls. From the coating room the rolls are sent to departments where the film is cut to the correct length and packaged. At all stages of manufacturing and storing, the sensitive film is kept at carefully controlled temperatures and protected from moisture in the air.

Developing Black and White Film

When a photographer snaps the shutter on his camera, a picture is recorded on the film. But the picture cannot yet be seen. Photographers call the invisible picture a latent, or hidden, image. The latent image is made up of hundreds of tiny silver specks on the silver-salt crystals. In order to bring out the latent image, the photographer must develop the film.

The photographer puts the film in a chemical solution that breaks down the silver salts until only the tiny bits of metallic silver that form the picture are left. Once the picture has appeared on the film, it is placed in a *stop bath*. The stop bath is really a rinse that washes off the developer and so stops its action on the silver salts. A third bath in a solution called a *hypo* permanently fixes the picture by getting rid of unexposed silver salts. Since the silver salts remain sensitive to light until the hypo has done its

Black and white shades are reversed on negatives. (The positive of this negative is on page 31.)

work, the photographer must develop his pictures in the dark. Developing is as much an art as taking pictures.

The film is now a *negative*. A negative has black and white shades reversed. A white house, for instance, comes out black, and a black coat looks white. That is because the picture is darker where the most light struck. The brighter light rays from the white house acted more strongly on the silver salts and left a heavier deposit of metallic silver than the rays from the black coat. To make the black and white shades true, the photographer makes a *positive* from the negative. He places the negative against another piece of paper coated with silver salts. When light is shone through the papers, the picture on the negative is copied on the second piece of paper, but this time the black and white shades appear as they naturally are.

Other Uses of Silver Salts

Photography is not the only use for silver salts. The crystals of silver iodine are the same shape as ice crystals. Silver-iodine crystals are dropped in clouds to form storms for areas that need rain. Silver nitrate is used as an antiseptic, as a backing for mirrors, and as a special ink that is brought out by light and is very difficult to erase. Because silver supplies are becoming so low, industries are trying to cut down their use of silver nitrate for these purposes.

A word of warning about silver salts needs to be given. All silver salts are highly poisonous and should only be handled by chemists who know how to use them.

The Best Conductor of Electricity

Electricity is a natural power. Man first discovered it in ancient times when he rubbed fur and saw sparks fly. But before man could put electricity to work for him, he had to find out how to store it and how to carry it from place to place. Hundreds of years passed before man was able to harness electricity.

During the eighteenth century, people were not sure what electricity was or how it could be created. They did learn that metals could carry an electric current, but they did not know what metals best carried the current or how to keep the current going. In 1786, an Italian, Luigi Galvani, noticed that as he dissected a dead frog, the frog twitched. Galvani decided to find out why the frog jumped and if he could make it jump again. He took the frog outside and hung it on a metal hook on his fence. He touched the frog with one metal after another and each time the frog jumped. Galvani found that the metal that made the frog jump most was silver. The only metal that could not make the frog jump was the same kind of metal as the hook. This should have told Galvani that it was the contact of the two different metals that generated the electricity, but he thought electricity in the frog itself made it jump.

Another Italian, Alessandro Volta, was sure the secret of electricity lay in the action of two metals. In 1800, Volta tested his idea and invented the first electric battery. The age of electricity had begun.

The complex electrical devices used today need the best con-

Silver coating on the springs of TV tuners help carry electric signals that tell the TV set what channel to receive. The long bars on the tuner are called tuning slugs. Each slug is sensitive to frequencies from only one station. When channels are switched, the proper tuning slug rotates into place. The buttons on the slug come into contact with the silver-coated springs and the picture and sound information for that channel are fed to the TV set. (Sylvania Electric Products, Inc.)

ductor of electricity, and that, scientists have discovered, is silver. The second greatest use of silver is in electricity. A battery made of silver and zinc is used today in guided missiles, jet planes, and some scientific instruments. The battery is lightweight but very powerful. It takes up little room, adds almost no weight, and produces the same energy as a battery many times its size. When the Explorer XVII satellite blasted into space, it was said to be carrying 150 pounds of silver-zinc batteries. Portable television cameras use batteries made of silver and cadmium. These are very heavy batteries, and they can stand a great deal of wear. The controls on fluorescent lamps are also made of silver. Each time you turn off a light, plug in a toaster, or start a vacuum cleaner, you may be relying on the power of silver to conduct electricity.

Many electrical contacts are made of silver because silver does not corrode and can withstand high temperatures. The silver is usually alloyed with copper, gold, and palladium. Silver-copper alloys are often used in electrical relays for computers and tabulators. The wires for the relays contain 72 percent silver and 28 percent copper. The relays help the computer carry and store information. Telephones also have silver in their relay systems. Silver has come to replace copper in many devices because copper corrodes faster than silver does. When copper corrodes, it builds up resistance at the contact point and its current-carrying ability is reduced. Even if a silver electrical contact corrodes, electricity can still move through it.

The number of uses of silver in electricity could be endless, but because silver is so scarce, technicians try to use it only where it is most needed. Most silver used in electricity goes into defense equipment, highly complex computers, and electrical devices that are used over and over again.

Computers help businessmen, scientists, and people in every walk of life get the information they need. Here, a man reviews a program for the computer to solve. Silver in the electrical circuits of the computer will carry the information on the typed sheet through the computer and help it gather together the requested facts. (General Electric Company)

Silver solder is put on machine parts that must hold together under extreme temperatures. The soldering gun is a complicated tool, and soldering is dangerous unless the technician is well protected. (American Welding Society)

Silver Has Many Uses

Because silver can withstand high temperatures and does not corrode easily, it is very important in soldering and brazing. Soldering and brazing are methods that join two metals together by dropping a melted substance called solder on the metals. As the solder hardens, it becomes very strong and holds the two metals tightly together. Silver solder is usually an alloy of silver with copper, zinc, tin, or cadmium. Silver solders are used in electrical appliances, air-conditioning units, and in the assembling of cars.

Honeycomb panels in the wings of jet airplanes are often held together by a solder of 95 percent silver and 5 percent aluminum.

Rocket nozzles have silver in them to prevent the nozzle from melting as it blasts off. Heavy-duty bearings in airplanes are made of silver alloys. The silver keeps the bearings from wearing out as they undergo sudden temperature changes and work at high speeds. Pure silver is added to bolts in equipment that has to stand the stress of high temperatures. If silver were not put in the bolts, they might stick together and be impossible to unscrew. Silver is put on copper parts that may have oxidized while in storage. The silver covering makes it easier to solder the oxidized parts together.

A silver compound is used to help coat ceramics. Silver oxide, another chemical compound, is used in chemical experiments to start different substances reacting with each other. Silver-oxide paint helps prevent iron from rusting. Fillings for teeth have long been a silver-tin alloy.

MINING AND REFINING SILVER

Silver is now rarely found by itself or in large amounts. It is usually mixed in with other metals and must be separated from these metals by refining. Over fifty different kinds of minerals have been found to contain silver, but the tiny deposits of silver are so scattered through the minerals that it is not practical to try to get them out. Only six silver-bearing ores are important. These ores contain large amounts of lead, zinc, copper, or gold, as well as silver. Sometimes all five metals are discovered in the same ore.

There are a few pure, or *native*, silver deposits in the world. One of the largest deposits of native silver was found in Kongs-

In a modern mine, miners are taken deep into the earth on a skip.
(Bunker Hill Company)

berg, Norway. One chunk of silver weighing over fifteen hundred pounds was dug out of the mines there. The famous "silver sidewalk" in Ontario, Canada, was a vein of native silver one block long and fifty feet wide. The silver sidewalk was dug up years ago. It is not likely that such rich deposits of silver will ever be found again.

Most silver ores lie in pockets in the earth or in long, narrow veins that run into the depths of a mountain. The only way to get the ore out is to dig a mine. From the very beginning of the history of silver, man has had to brave the dangers of cave-ins and explosions from gas trapped in the mine. He has had to dig his way through miles of rocks and dirt to find a vein of silver ore only a few inches wide. He has had to breathe air filled with poisonous fumes, and he has had to work in blazing heat. But man has been willing to undergo all these dangers because silver is so important to him.

Silver Strikes

For many years people thought they had found all the silver in the world. They took silver from the mines of Spain, Mexico, and Peru, but they did not try to find new supplies of silver. Then, a series of accidents opened up untouched and rich veins of silver ore.

In 1750, in New South Wales, Australia, a settler was trying to find new supplies of tin that he needed to mend pans and to make utensils for his home. Instead of tin, he found a fabulous supply of silver at Broken Hills, a place so named because of its strange shape. His discovery soon made Australia an important producer of silver.

The richest silver ore in the world appeared to be worthless

Cutout of the Comstock Mine being worked in 1876. (Culver Pictures, Inc.)

black rock to the two men who discovered it in Nevada. The date was 1859, just ten years after the first discovery of gold brought thousands of gold hunters to western United States. The men were Peter O'Riley and Patrick McLaughlin, and they were looking for gold in the Sierra Nevada mountains. They found rock that had bits of gold in it, dug out the gold, and threw the rest of the rock away.

Another man thought the black rock looked very interesting, and he took a sample back across the mountains to California, where he asked an expert to examine the rock. For every ton of rock, the expert said, there was about a thousand dollars' worth of gold. That was a great deal of gold. But the real discovery was that the ore was loaded with silver — every ton of ore had about three thousand dollars' worth of silver in it. The silver stampede was on.

The ore came from what was to become the famous Ophir Mine of the Comstock Lode in Nevada. Soon the former gold hunters from California were heading for the Comstock Lode. To get there, they had to cross the Rocky Mountains. The people were so excited by the dream of discovering more silver that they dared anything. Mountain trails where one stumble would send a man plunging into a canyon did not stop them. Neither did blizzards nor a shortage of horses. If a stagecoach was full, people went on by foot. By spring, hundreds of people had poured into the boom-town of Virginia City.

Virginia City itself was a sorry sight. The "homes" the miners built were simply tents made out of potato sacks and old blankets. Men slept three to a bed in the town's boardinghouse.

Mining at the nearby Comstock Lode was no easy matter either. The best silver was far down in the ground, and it took a team of men to dig the tunnels and bring out the ore. Only a well-organized mining company could manage such an operation. Soon the fortune hunters had either sold their claims to the Comstock Mining Company or had gone to work for it.

As the miners dug deeper and deeper into the earth, temperatures rose higher and higher. It was so hot that the miners could only work a few hours at a time. Then in 1863, at the level of three thousand feet, a wall broke in the mine. Water as hot as 170 degrees poured into the mine and all the miners who could rushed to safety. To get the mine working again, the owners dug a tunnel five miles long to drain off the water. Once again, the miners went

In the late nineteenth century, mule-drawn wagons carried the silver across the mountains to refineries in San Francisco.

down into the mine. Now the temperature was 120 degrees, and the air was filled with sulfur fumes. The tunnel had not worked. The lower levels of the mine had to be closed even though there was still silver there.

The mine owners did not really care that parts of the Comstock Lode had to be closed off. One owner was already so rich he had solid silver knobs on every door of his house. More important, the Comstock Lode brought Nevada one step closer to statehood. Nevada was still part of Utah Territory. The citizens of Nevada sent silver bars along with a delegation to Washington, D.C., to prove to the President that Nevada was strong and rich enough to be a territory. President Abraham Lincoln believed they were right. In 1861, Nevada became a territory, and in 1864, a state.

The heyday of the Comstock Lode was not yet over. In 1873, a seam of silver more than 50 feet thick was discovered in the Comstock. It came to be known as the Big Bonanza. For the next twenty years, the Comstock Lode produced millions of dollars' worth of silver and gold.

Silver Strikes in Other States

Silver strikes were made not only in Nevada but in Colorado, Idaho, and Arizona, as well. In 1876, rich supplies of silver ore were found in the worked-out gold mines of Leadville, Colorado. Leadville had become a ghost town after the gold miners left it. Two years after the discovery of silver the town had grown from a shabby nest of twenty shanties to a thriving town with a population of 35,000. Leadville continued to be a center of silver mining for many years.

Legend has it that the last fabulous deposit of silver was found by a miner's donkey. In 1885, a tired and discouraged miner was riding along a trail on a borrowed donkey. The donkey stepped on a rock and crushed it. As the miner looked down, he saw, much to his surprise, that silver dust was scattered all over the ground. The donkey had discovered silver from the silver seams in the Coeur d'Alene district of Idaho. The miner claimed the find as his, but the donkey's owner demanded that he get a part of the claim because it was his donkey that made the discovery. The court agreed with him and awarded him a share of the land.

The Coeur d'Alene district turned out to be very rich in silver, lead, zinc, and gold. Today, mines in this district still produce most of the silver in the United States.

Silver Mining Today

The leading silver producers in the world today are Mexico, Peru, the United States, Canada, the Soviet Union, and Australia. In the United States, four states (Idaho, Arizona, Utah, and Montana) lead in the production of silver. Since the Comstock Lode mines are no longer in operation, silver production has dropped in Nevada. Colorado's supply has also gone down.

Ores are no longer mined to obtain just one metal. Of the twenty-four leading silver mines in the United States, only four mine silver alone. The other twenty-one take copper, lead, gold, arsenic, antimony, zinc, and other valuable by-products from the ore.

Silver mining has changed greatly from the old days. Modern equipment allows the miners to work in safety and comfort no matter how deep into the ground they go. In the Bunker Hill Mine in the Coeur d'Alene district, the miners start work at 3,600 feet above sea level. During the day the miner may go as much as a mile deeper into the earth until he is 2,000 feet *below* sea level.

Pillars of low-grade ore support this section of a silver mine. The loader in the background is scooping up blasted-out ore. (Bunker Hill Company)

A visitor touring the whole mine would have to travel more than a hundred miles. Because the mine is so big, it is divided into levels. Elevators take the men from one level to another.

Today the air is pure even in the lowest level of a mine. In the Bunker Hill Mine, a pumping system sends 150,000 cubic feet of air per minute into the mine. To keep the mine free of water, another pumping system takes 1,300 gallons of water out of the mine every minute.

Railroad cars carry the miners to the work area and transport ore back to the main center, where it is loaded onto a gigantic hoisting machine and lifted to the top of the mine.

Picks and shovels are no longer used. Instead, trained men place explosives in the rock. The ore is blasted out and machines called muckers scoop the ore up and load it onto the cars.

There is always danger from cave-ins, and miners must support the dug-out areas. They use two methods to support the blasted-out rock. One method is called *timbered cut and fill*. As the men cut through the rock, they put in heavy timbers to keep the tunnel from falling in. The method is used in places where the ore is *high grade*, that is, rich in silver and other metals. When the ore is not very rich, they use the second method, or *pillar stopping*. Instead of bringing in timbers, the miners leave blocks of ore as columns to hold up the ceiling of the mine. When an area has been completely worked out, it is filled with sand so that it cannot collapse.

Miner using a drill to set the explosive that will take out high-grade lead–silver ore.

(Bunker Hill Company)

Refining Silver

Silver is refined by separating it from its ores. The ore must go through many steps before the pure silver can be taken out. Each of these steps is based upon the way different metals and chemicals react to each other. Today a person who knows chemistry can easily understand what each of the steps do and why they are necessary. But hundreds of years of experience lie behind the modern knowledge of chemistry.

Imagine the surprise and delight of the first person who successfully refined silver. The time was somewhere around 3000 B.C., and man's only tools were fire and polished stone. He did not know about iron, and he had not yet invented the wheel. But he had found copper and lead ores.

Both copper and lead ores contain silver, but the refining processes for the two ores are not the same. Silver was first refined from lead ores by a process that we call *cupellation*. For some unknown but lucky reason, man heated lead ores. Heating, of course, is the

An engraving from the Middle Ages shows chemists refining silver by cuppelation. The man at right is forcing air into the pot with bellows.

key to many refining processes. As the lead ore melted from the heat, air blew through the ore. Suddenly, a bead of silver appeared. Early people thought the lead had magically turned to silver. They did not understand that a chemical change in the lead ore had taken place. Lead oxidizes easily. Because silver does not oxidize easily, it remains in the ore pot after the lead has been oxidized.

Once man discovered that heating lead ores and blowing air through the ores "created" silver, he began to improve the process. At first he put the ore in a sloping trench so that air could reach it. Then he learned to build furnaces for the ore and to make mechanical air blowers. These were called bellows and were pumped full of air by hand. The Incas did not have bellows. Instead, they put their ore pots on mountainsides where the winds blew through the bubbling mass of melted ore.

One of the favorite metals of these early scientists was mercury. They were fascinated by the silvery liquid that could turn into a metal, and they called it quicksilver. Soon these men discovered that if they added mercury to melted silver ore, the silver combined with mercury and could be skimmed off. They could easily separate the mercury from the silver by heating the compound until the mercury evaporated. This new method was called *amalgamation* and was very popular until the chemists found out that cyanide separates silver from its ores as well as mercury does. *Cyanidation* soon replaced amalgamation and is still in use in some parts of the world.

Refining Silver Today

Refining processes must meet the industrial demand for all kinds of metals and minerals. Ores are refined so thoroughly that nothing

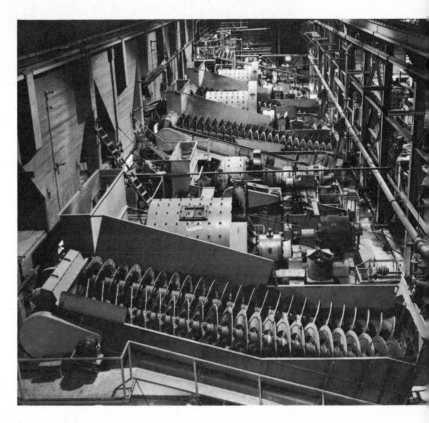

The interior of a refinery today is a far cry from the refining techniques of the Middle Ages. These large machines grind and concentrate the ore. (Bunker Hill Company)

is wasted. Even the gas from the refining furnace is cleaned, and any valuable by-products are collected from the gas and used.

The first step in removing silver from its ore is to break up the large pieces of ore that have come from the mine. This is known as milling or *concentrating* the ore. The first operation takes place in a ball mill, where dozens of steel balls, each weighing about ten tons, tumble against the ore. Lumps ranging up to a foot in size are reduced to one-inch pieces. Next, the ore is tested to see how rich it is in silver, gold, lead, and zinc, and then, in the final

Silver combines with lead and rises in frothy bubbles to the top of the flotation tank. (Bunker Hill Company)

grounding, it is powdered into bits about the size of sugar grains to ready it for refining.

While the ore is in the ball mill, chemicals that help the different metals in the ore separate from each other are mixed in. The first separation takes place in the flotation tank. There silver, gold, and other metals combine with lead and rise to the top of the tank as a frothy mass to be skimmed off. The ore is now called a concentrate and is very rich.

The leftover ore is moved on to the zinc flotation tank where the same process is repeated. The material left in the tank is called *tailings*. After cleaning, it is pumped into the mine to fill in mined-out areas.

Skimming off a silver-and-zinc compound from a 235-ton refining kettle. (Bunker Hill Company)

The concentrated ore is roasted and placed in a blast furnace where the ore separates once again. After this separation the material is called *lead bullion*. Copper, then arsenic, and finally antimony are removed from the bullion at the lead refinery.

Gold and silver are separated from the remaining lead bullion by adding zinc. The gold and silver unite with the zinc and are

Weighing 1,200-ounce troy bar. (Bunker Hill Company)

skimmed off. The zinc is removed by distillation, any remaining lead by cupellation, and at last the gold and silver are separated. *Electrolysis* is often used to separate silver from copper and gold ores. An electric current is passed through the specially conditioned ores until the metals in the ores separate from each other and the silver collects around one of the electric poles.

The pure silver is cast into 1,200-ounce troy bars for marketing. Troy is a special weight system used for gold and silver.

SILVER'S FUTURE

The future of silver is both promising and frightening. Each technical advance seems to bring another use for silver. For instance, a new type of glass containing silver salts is being developed. The glass will give excellent protection against the damaging rays and heat of the sun. Think how much more an astronomer might discover if he could study the sun more directly without danger to his eyes. Space flights could go so much closer to the sun if such a glass could shield the astronauts from radiation. But will there be enough silver for this glass and for the other devices that depend so heavily on silver?

It has been estimated that the supply of silver will last from fourteen to twenty-one years at the present rate of production. Right now, the United States uses nearly four times as much silver as it mines. Silver from the government's stockpile and purchases of silver from other countries make up the difference. The stockpile cannot last for many more years, and other countries do not have unlimited supplies of silver. Where then will the world find its silver?

A cart of silver bars ready for industrial use. (Bunker Hill Company)

The picture is not entirely bleak. By cutting down the amount of silver in coins, the government has tried to save its silver supply. Even though industry uses a great deal of silver, it does not always use it up. In spite of the fact that research laboratories have not yet found a substitute for the greatest use of silver, photographic emulsion, the photographic industry does try to protect its silver supply. About 50 percent of the silver for black and white photographs and 90 percent of the silver in color photographs are recovered and used again. Moreover, silver is not used for Xerox or polaroid processes and this may be one way to cut down on the heavy use of silver in the field of photography. Silver that goes into jewelry and tableware can last for thousands of years if it is properly cared for. However, silver in a rocket nozzle is probably lost forever. Silver used in electrical appliances is also difficult to recover. The importance of silver as a conductor of electricity is growing, and so far no substitute has been found that carries current so well and withstands heat and temperature change at the same time. Experts are searching for materials that can be substituted for silver in soldering and minor industrial uses such as backing for mirrors. A new filling for teeth has been developed that contains no silver, but it is not yet as satisfactory as a silver filling.

There is still silver in the earth. Most of the deposits of silver lie in copper, lead, and zinc ores. Even though mining companies may have a small market for lead and zinc, they are almost certain to continue mining these ores for their silver content. There are also tiny deposits of silver scattered in other ores throughout the world. In the past it has not been worthwhile to mine such small deposits, but better mining techniques and the shortage of silver should make it possible and profitable to mine these low-grade ores.

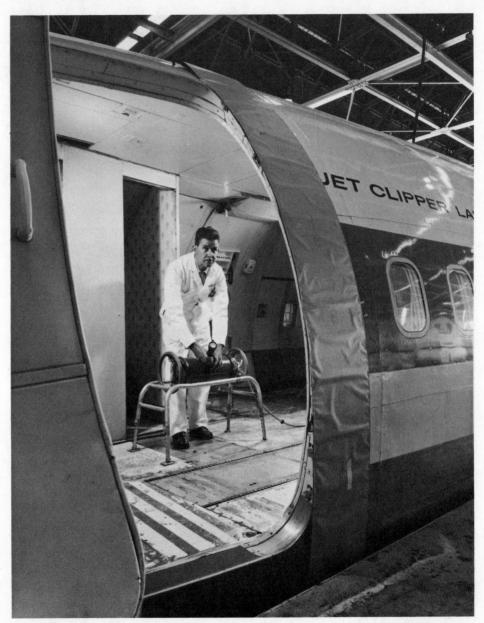

A technician using x-ray equipment to make a film to check for flaws in a plane. The honeycomb panels in a jet are soldered together with a silver alloy, and the bearings have silver in them.

Whatever means man uses to solve his need for silver, one thing is certain. Silver is likely to be as important to man's future as it has been to his past.

INDEX